TOOLS FOR CAREGIVERS

- **F&P LEVEL:** A
- **WORD COUNT:** 26
- **CURRICULUM CONNECTIONS:** animals, habitats, nature

Skills to Teach

- **HIGH-FREQUENCY WORDS:** a, an, I, see
- **CONTENT WORDS:** baby, claws, eye, iguana, scales, spikes, tail
- **PUNCTUATION:** exclamation points, periods
- **WORD STUDY:** /k/, spelled c (claws, scales); long /a/, spelled ai (tail); long /e/, spelled ee (see); long /e/, spelled y (baby)
- **TEXT TYPE:** information report

Before Reading Activities

- Read the title and give a simple statement of the main idea.
- Have students "walk" through the book and talk about what they see in the pictures.
- Introduce new vocabulary by having students predict the first letter and locate the word in the text.
- Discuss any unfamiliar concepts that are in the text.

After Reading Activities

Explain to readers that iguanas are reptiles. Show readers pictures of other reptiles. What does each reptile have in common? How are they different from mammals, like dogs, and birds, like parrots? Show readers pictures of all animal classes. Identify their differences together. What animal class do readers like best? Why?

Tadpole Books are published by Jump!, 5357 Penn Avenue South, Minneapolis, MN 55419, www.jumplibrary.com

Copyright ©2024 Jump. International copyright reserved in all countries. No part of this book may be reproduced in any form without written permission from the publisher.

Editor: Jenna Gleisner **Designer:** Emma Almgren-Bersie

Photo Credits: Christine C Brooks/Shutterstock, cover; fivespots/Shutterstock, 1; agefotostock/Alamy, 2tl, 14–15; asiadomaga/Shutterstock, 2tr, 10–11; Fery Fernady/iStock, 2ml, 4–5; Sutthichai Somthong/Shutterstock, 2mr, 6–7; Matthew Ragen/Dreamstime, 2bl, 8–9; dwi putra stock/Shutterstock, 2br, 12–13; Milan Zygmunt/Shutterstock, 3; Ricardod89/Shutterstock, 16tl; Kurit afshen/Shutterstock, 16tr; Lauren Suryanata/Shutterstock, 16bl; Isabellebonaire/Dreamstime, 16br.

Library of Congress Cataloging-in-Publication Data
Names: Deniston, Natalie, author.
Title: Iguanas / by Natalie Deniston.
Description: Minneapolis, MN: Jump!, Inc., (2024)
Series: My first animal books | Includes index.
Audience: Ages 3–6
Identifiers: LCCN 2022054066 (print)
LCCN 2022054067 (ebook)
ISBN 9798885246644 (hardcover)
ISBN 9798885246651 (paperback)
ISBN 9798885246668 (ebook)
Subjects: LCSH: Iguanas—Juvenile literature.
Classification: LCC QL666.L25 D46 2024 (print)
LCC QL666.L25 (ebook)
DDC 597.95/42—dc23/eng/20221110
LC record available at https://lccn.loc.gov/2022054066
LC ebook record available at https://lccn.loc.gov/2022054067

MY FIRST ANIMAL BOOKS

IGUANAS

by Natalie Deniston

TABLE OF CONTENTS

Words to Know	2
Iguanas	3
Let's Review!	16
Index	16

WORDS TO KNOW

baby

claws

eye

scales

spikes

tail

IGUANAS

I see an iguana!

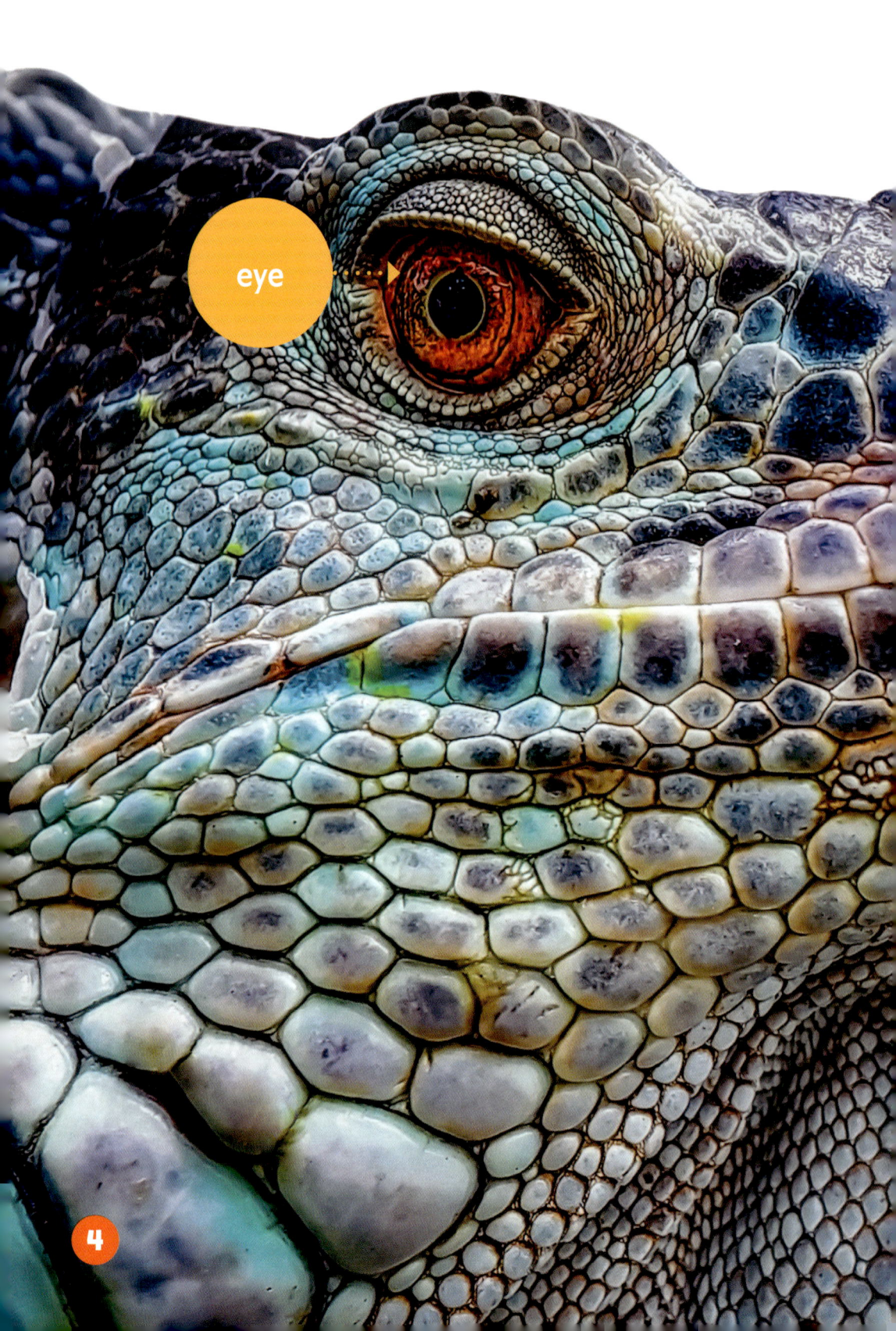

I see an eye.

scales

I see scales.

I see spikes.

I see claws.

tail

I see a tail.

baby iguana

I see a baby!

LET'S REVIEW!

Iguanas are reptiles. They can be different colors. What color is each iguana below?

INDEX

baby 15

claws 11

eye 5

scales 7

spikes 9

tail 13